ABRAHAM

LINCOLN

GREAT AMERICAN PRESIDENT

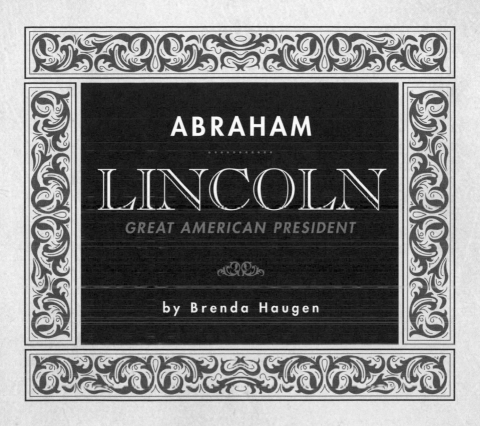

ABRAHAM
LINCOLN
GREAT AMERICAN PRESIDENT

by Brenda Haugen

Content Adviser: Barbara J. Sanders, M.A.,
Education Specialist
Gettysburg National Military Park

Reading Adviser: Rosemary G. Palmer, Ph.D.,
Department of Literacy, College of Education,
Boise State University

COMPASS POINT BOOKS MINNEAPOLIS, MINNESOTA

Compass Point Books
3109 West 50th Street, #115
Minneapolis, MN 55410

Visit Compass Point Books on the Internet at *www.compasspointbooks.com*
or e-mail your request to *custserv@compasspointbooks.com*

Editor: Heidi Schoof
Lead Designer: Jaime Martens
Photo Researchers: Bobbie Nuytten and Marcie C. Spence
Page Production: Bobbie Nuytten
Cartographer: XNR Productions, Inc.
Educational Consultant: Diane Smolinski

Managing Editor: Catherine Neitge
Creative Director: Keith Griffin
Editorial Director: Carol Jones

To Martha and Sylvester Heitkamp. I adore you both! BLH

Library of Congress Cataloging-in-Publication Data
Haugen, Brenda.
  Abraham Lincoln : great American President / by Brenda Haugen.
    p. cm.—(Signature lives)
  Includes bibliographical references and index.
  ISBN 0-7565-0986-6 (hardcover)
  1. Lincoln, Abraham, 1809–1865—Juvenile literature. 2. Presidents—
United States—Biography—Juvenile literature. I. Title. II. Series.
  E457.905.H298 2006
  973.7'092—dc22   2005009097

Signature Lives

CIVIL WAR ERA

The Civil War (1861–1865) split the United States into two countries and divided the people over the issue of slavery The opposing sides—the Union in the North and the Confederacy in the South—battled each other for four long years in the deadliest American conflict ever fought. The bloody war sometimes pitted family members and friends against each other over the issues of slavery and states' rights. Some of the people who lived and served their country during the Civil War are among the nation's most beloved heroes.

Abraham Lincoln

Table of Contents

"Forever Free" 9

Growing Up on the Frontier 15

Striking Out on His Own 29

Family Man 39

Battling Against Douglas 49

Mr. President 59

Conviction and Controversy 69

Assassination 81

Legacy 93

Life and Times 96
Life at a Glance 102
Additional Resources 103
Glossary 105
Source Notes 106
Select Bibliography 108
Index 109
Image Credits 112

Chapter

1 "FOREVER FREE"

❧❦❧

Early on the morning of New Year's Day, 1863, President Abraham Lincoln sat at his desk putting the finishing touches on a soon-to-be-historic document. Lincoln was tired. He had tossed and turned all night as he considered the final wording of his official Emancipation Proclamation.

Nothing in his life had prepared Abraham Lincoln to lead a nation now entering its third year of bloody civil war. Still, as president, Lincoln stood firm on his main goal—to preserve the Union. It broke his heart to see his beloved countrymen dying on the battlefields as the war dragged on. He had offered the South every opportunity—first to avoid war and then to bring the war to a close—but nothing worked. The time to act was now.

Abraham Lincoln is remembered as the Great Emancipator, the man who freed the slaves.

President Lincoln spent most of that morning shaking hands at the White House's traditional New Year's reception. Toward the end of the party, Lincoln and several of his Cabinet members retired to the president's office for the final signing of the Emancipation Proclamation.

Before signing, Lincoln read once more the words proclaiming that "all persons held as slaves within any State ... in rebellion against the United States, should be then, thenceforward, and forever free."

The decision to free all slaves in the rebellious Southern states had not come easily. Abraham Lincoln was a man who watched, waited, and thought long and hard about every issue. He liked to turn things over and over in his mind before reaching a decision. By approaching a situation from every angle and considering every detail, Lincoln often saw things that others had completely overlooked.

By far the toughest decision Abraham Lincoln ever had to face was the one he had to make about slavery. As a young congressman from Illinois, Lincoln had remained quiet as others hotly debated the issue.

In the South, wealthy plantation owners claimed a "sacred right" to own African-Americans as slaves. And although most Southerners owned no slaves at all, they agreed that slavery was right and proper. They believed that blacks were by nature inferior and needed to be ruled by whites.

In the North, the abolitionist movement was growing, but only a handful of people actually believed blacks were equal to whites and deserved the same freedoms. Most abolitionists simply believed that slavery was wrong, and should not be allowed. They didn't think ahead to what would happen if all the slaves were freed.

Abraham Lincoln meets with members of his Cabinet for a reading of the Emancipation Proclamation.

Although African-Americans in the Northern states were "free," they were not considered equal to whites. Most states had laws stating what African-Americans could and could not do. In Lincoln's state of Illinois, "free" African-Americans were required to pay taxes; however they were not allowed to vote, hold political office, attend schools, serve on juries, or even testify in court.

Most jobs were denied to free blacks as well. Many became indentured servants. They signed contracts to work for a set number of years without wages, in exchange for food, clothing, and shelter.

Abraham Lincoln was one of a large number of Northerners who opposed slavery, but were willing to let it be, as long as it stayed in the South. Lincoln did not think that Congress had the power to interfere with slavery in states where it already existed. He hoped that by passing laws to keep slavery from spreading into new territories, Congress would eventually force the "natural death" of slavery in the South.

By the time Abraham Lincoln was elected president in 1860, it was obvious that slavery was not just going to fade away. Southerners hated and feared the idea of an antislavery Republican in the White House. Southern states began to secede, or break away, from the Union.

Lincoln tried to find a way to keep the nation together. He studied the history of the United States and the words and writings of the Founding Fathers. As the Civil War raged, Lincoln thought long and hard to understand how a nation founded on the idea of

In 1857, a Supreme Court ruling known as the Dred Scott decision declared that African-American slaves were not citizens of the United States. Instead, they were considered private property. While the Dred Scott decision was a major setback for those in the fight against slavery, it also shocked many others into joining the cause.

democracy had come to be split so horribly in two.

In the end, Lincoln realized that slavery had been the issue all along. The Declaration of Independence states that all men are created equal, and that all are therefore entitled to the same rights and freedoms.

From his humble boyhood on the American frontier, Lincoln had worked hard and taken every opportunity he was given to make something of himself. He believed that every man, black or white, rich or poor, should be allowed that same opportunity.

And so, on January 1, 1863, Lincoln picked up a gold pen to put his official signature on the Emancipation Proclamation. The president normally signed his name "A. Lincoln." On this day, however, he carefully wrote out his full name, remarking, "If my name ever goes into history, it will be for this act." ஃ

2 GROWING UP ON THE FRONTIER

❦

Abraham Lincoln grew up poor on the American frontier. He was named after his grandfather, who had moved to Kentucky in the early 1780s on the advice of Daniel Boone, a distant relative. Tempted by tales of rich farmland, Grandpa Abe sold his farm in Virginia and, together with his wife and five children, headed over the mountains to Kentucky.

Located on the western frontier, Kentucky was a wild land of unpredictable weather, vicious animals, and occasionally dangerous American Indians. In the spring of 1786, Grandpa Abe was shot and killed by hostile Native Americans while planting a field of corn with his three sons.

The eldest son, 15-year-old Mordecai, ordered his brother Josiah to seek help in the nearest com-

Abraham Lincoln enjoyed a lifelong love of reading. Without electricity or money for lamps, young Abraham read by firelight.

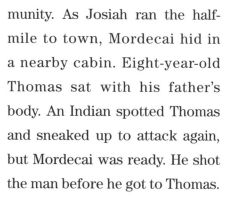

munity. As Josiah ran the half-mile to town, Mordecai hid in a nearby cabin. Eight-year-old Thomas sat with his father's body. An Indian spotted Thomas and sneaked up to attack again, but Mordecai was ready. He shot the man before he got to Thomas.

Thomas, who would grow up to be the father of President Abraham Lincoln, inherited nothing when his father died. According to the law, Mordecai, as the oldest son, was entitled to everything his father had owned.

Though Thomas Lincoln grew up without an education, he was respected for his honesty and willingness to work. A short, stocky man who loved to swap stories, Thomas worked at farming, carpentry, cabinet-making, and other jobs he found in nearby Hodgenville and Elizabethtown. Thomas saved the money he earned and used it to buy his own farm on Mill Creek in Hardin County, Kentucky.

In 1806, Thomas married Nancy Hanks. Nancy's family had moved from Virginia to Kentucky around 1780. Although they were respectable farmers who made a decent living, most of them never learned to read. Nancy may have been an exception. Historians

believe she could read but couldn't write. Nancy was a talented seamstress who found work sewing everything from wedding gowns to funeral clothes.

Settlers and Native Americans clashed over land on the Kentucky frontier.

With a new wife and a baby on the way, Thomas built a little house in Elizabethtown, Kentucky. Soon after the home was finished, Nancy gave birth to their first child, a daughter named Sarah.

In 1809, Thomas bought a 300-acre (120-hectare) farm on Nolin Creek near Hodgenville, Kentucky. There he built a one-room log cabin measuring 16 feet by 18 feet (4.8 meters by 5.5 meters). With a dirt floor and no glass windows, the cabin looked much

Mrs. Lincoln's spinning jenny sits by the fireplace in the cabin where Abraham Lincoln was born.

like other pioneer homes in the area. It was here, on February 12, 1809, that Nancy and Thomas Lincoln welcomed their son Abraham into the world.

Before Abraham turned 2, the family moved again. This time Thomas purchased a smaller farm on better land about 10 miles (16 kilometers) to the northeast, on Knob Creek. A son the Lincolns named Thomas was born here, but he died as a baby.

As a young child, Abraham was expected to help out wherever he could. While his father planted corn in the field, Abraham followed behind, dropping pumpkin seeds along the way. He also helped with the harvest when the crops were ready to pick.

But life wasn't all work for young Abraham. The boy loved to fish and play games, and usually found time to do so. He also liked school, but getting there was difficult. The nearest school was a windowless log cabin about two miles (three km) from the Lincoln home. It was called a "blab school," because the students learned their lessons by reciting them aloud. Although Abraham and his sister, Sarah, walked to school whenever possible, Lincoln's total schooling amounted to less than one year.

By the time Abraham turned 7, his father decided he'd had enough of Kentucky. Thomas Lincoln never liked the fact that slavery was legal in the state. He was also concerned about boundary conflicts.

Kentucky settlers set their own boundaries for their land, often using stones, trees, and other natural materials as boundary markers. When new settlers moved in and raised boundary disputes, the people already living on and working the land found they had a difficult time proving ownership. Without the help of a lawyer, many of the original settlers lost their land. Thomas knew that if he were ever called into court, he wouldn't be able to afford a lawyer. He thought it best if he moved his family to a place where land ownership was clear. He chose to seek his fortune in Indiana.

In the fall of 1816, just a few months before Indiana officially became a state, Thomas journeyed into the wilderness to claim a plot of land. He found what he was looking for in a heavily wooded area along Little Pigeon Creek.

Thomas built a small, three-sided shelter of logs and branches and marked his property with burned brush. He then headed back to Kentucky to collect his family and their few belongings.

On a cold December morning, the Lincolns set off together on a 100-mile (160-km) journey to their new home. The last six or seven miles of the trip were the most difficult. Thomas had to cut through trees and tangled underbrush so his family could get through.

Seven-year-old Abraham found his Indiana home a bit scary at first. Until Thomas finished building a proper log house, the family stayed in the 14-foot by 14-foot (4-m by 4-m) shelter he'd originally built. Through the winter, the family kept a fire burning at the open end of the shelter. The fire helped to keep them warm and scared away bears, wolves, and other wild animals that filled the surrounding woods.

Even when the cabin was completed, it proved far from perfect. Because Thomas built the home in the cold winter months, the clay and grass used to seal the cracks between the logs didn't set properly. Wailing winter winds whipped through the house.

The cracks also allowed spaces through which young Abraham could aim and shoot his rifle, which he did—once. Around his eighth birthday, Abraham

One of young
Abraham's
chores was
cutting wood
for his mother.

looked through a space in the cabin's wall and spied a turkey outside. After grabbing his rifle, Abraham fired a shot from inside his home. Seeing the turkey fall down dead, Abraham felt awful. It was the last time he hunted anything.

In the spring, Abraham helped his father clear the land in order to plant crops. Abraham was big for an 8-year-old and strong enough to handle an ax.

Life in Indiana proved even tougher than life in

Abraham Lincoln was 7 years old when his family built and moved into this Indiana log home.

Kentucky. Since their home lay in such a remote area, the Lincolns had to be independent, raising everything they needed to survive. All the family members had chores. For Abraham, these included taking care of the farm animals before breakfast.

Though a few other families lived nearby, life in Indiana was lonely at first. In the fall of 1817, Nancy's aunt and uncle joined the Lincolns, and the family grew happier. Thomas and Elizabeth Sparrow brought with them their adopted son, Dennis Hanks, who became a big brother to Abraham and served as an extra hand around the farm.

When Abraham was about 9 years old, his father trusted him to travel the two miles (three km) to the nearest gristmill, where the family's crop of corn could be ground into meal. Wary of wild animals, young Abraham desperately wanted to get home before dark. In his rush, Abraham decided to hurry the horse that turned the mill's wheel. Each time around, Abraham cracked the horse with a whip until the animal became angry and kicked him in the head.

People at the mill saw what had happened and thought Abraham was dead. They ran to alert Thomas, who discovered Abraham still alive but unable to speak. Within hours, however, Abraham started talking. Later, he fully recovered.

Although the Lincolns had avoided one tragedy, another soon followed—the death of Abraham's mother, Nancy.

On the frontier, farm animals were rarely penned in. Cows often wandered in the woods and ate whatever greens they could find. Unknown to the Lincolns and their neighbors, a poisonous plant called white snakeroot grew abundantly in the nearby forest. People became deathly ill from drinking the poisoned milk of cows that had

Thomas Lincoln, Abraham's father

Map showing the Great Lakes region including Wisconsin, Michigan, Canada, New York, Iowa, Illinois, Indiana, Ohio, Pennsylvania, Virginia, West Virginia, Kentucky, Tennessee, North Carolina, and locations related to Lincoln's life.

Abraham Lincoln lived in many different places during his lifetime.

eaten this plant.

When Tom and Betsy Sparrow got sick, Nancy went to take care of them until they got better. After suffering chills, fever, dizziness and upset stomachs, the Sparrows eventually died. The only thing Nancy could do was offer comfort in their final hours.

By the time Nancy came home, she, too, felt dizzy and ill. Knowing she was about to die, she called Abraham and Sarah to her bedside. Nancy made the children promise to be good and kind to people and to help their father. Nancy Hanks Lincoln died on October 5, 1818, at the age of 34.

Despite their grief, the Lincoln family carried on. Eleven-year-old Sarah took over all the chores her mother had done. She worked hard to keep the house clean, but sometimes sadness overcame her, and she simply sat in front of the fire and cried.

As a skilled carpenter, Thomas Lincoln was called upon to make coffins for those who died. Thomas himself made the coffin in which his wife's body would be placed. Young Abraham carved the pegs that held the coffin together.

Nine-year-old Abraham reacted differently to his mother's death. He wouldn't even talk about it. The loss made him more sensitive to other people's feelings. Years later, he recalled the death of his mother when he wrote a letter to a child who'd also lost a loved one. He wrote:

> *In this sad world of ours, sorrow comes to all; and, to the young, it comes with bitterest agony, because it takes them unawares. I have had experience enough to know what I say.*

The Lincolns' lonely days ended in 1819 when Sarah Bush Johnston and her three children joined the family. Thomas had known Sarah during his

> *In 1826, Abraham's sister, Sarah, married a neighbor named Aaron Grigsby. Just three weeks before her 21st birthday, Sarah died while giving birth to their child, a stillborn baby boy. Abraham, who was 18 at the time, never forgave Grigsby. He believed Sarah died because Grigsby did not call for a doctor soon enough.*

bachelor days in Kentucky. He met her again on a trip back to Elizabethtown one year after Nancy's death. Their courtship was more like a business deal than a love affair. Sarah was a widow, and Thomas needed a mother for his children. Thomas promised to pay her debts and provide a home for her in Indiana if Sarah agreed to marry him.

Right from the start, Sarah showed compassion for the Lincoln children. Abraham and Sarah, in return, grew to adore their stepmother and her young children, Elizabeth, John, and Matilda. Sarah and her children brought love and laughter back into the Lincoln household.

In addition to her love, Sarah Bush Johnston brought cleanliness and order to the home. She cleaned, organized, and oversaw a number of improvements to the cabin.

"She soaped—rubbed and washed the children clean, so that they look[ed] pretty neat—well and clean," one Lincoln relative remembered.

Sarah Bush Johnston also encouraged her stepchildren to learn to read and write. Though

Abraham attended school only a few weeks each winter, he continued to learn throughout his childhood, mostly through reading. He read anything he could get his hands on, including the family Bible and books about George Washington, Benjamin Franklin, and American history. Through his books, Abraham was able to dream of a life beyond the frontier.

Sarah Bush Johnston, Lincoln's beloved stepmother

Sarah was impressed by her stepson's desire to learn. She encouraged Abraham to keep reading and working toward his dreams. She said:

> *He must understand every thing—even to the smallest thing—minutely and exactly. He would then repeat it over to himself again and again—some times in one form and then in another and when it was fixed in his mind to suit him he … never lost that fact or his understanding of it.* ✒

3 STRIKING OUT ON HIS OWN

❧

As the years passed, Abraham grew taller and taller. By age 16, Abraham stood 6 feet 2 inches (188 centimeters) tall but weighed only 160 pounds (72 kilograms). Nevertheless, work on the frontier made him strong. He was one of the best wrestlers and runners around. Before he turned 20, Abraham would reach his full height of 6 feet 4 inches (193 cm), very tall for a man in his day.

To help support his large family, Thomas Lincoln hired Abraham out to other farmers who needed help. Abraham earned 25 cents a day digging wells, splitting fence rails, cutting down trees, and building pigpens. The money Abraham earned went back to his family.

Although it probably wasn't his fault, as a teenager Abraham earned a reputation for being lazy.

Lincoln the Rail Splitter *was painted by renowned artist Jean Leon Gerome Ferris.*

His body was growing so quickly that he almost always felt tired. As a result, Thomas and Abraham began to argue, and Abraham dreamed of the day when he'd be able to go out on his own.

Abraham got his chance after he turned 19. In the spring of 1828, merchant James Gentry hired Abraham to go with his son Allen on a 1,200-mile (1,920-km) voyage by flatboat to New Orleans, Louisiana. Their job was to deliver a cargo of meat, corn, and flour. Gentry gave Abraham and Allen a great deal of responsibility. The young men were expected to protect the goods throughout the trip, sell them in the city, and return with the money. Abraham and Allen promised not to let Mr. Gentry down.

With the goods loaded on the boat, Abraham and Allen floated down the Ohio and Mississippi rivers until they reached New Orleans. Looking around, Abraham couldn't believe his eyes. He'd never before seen a city the size of New Orleans. In the harbor, the boys heard strange languages spoken and saw ships from ports all over the world. They watched with fascination as women in beautiful gowns strolled along the streets.

But not everything in New Orleans was beautiful. For the first time in his life, Abraham saw slaves being sold on the auction block. Prospective buyers looked over the slaves in the same way they checked out animals for sale. Abraham was deeply

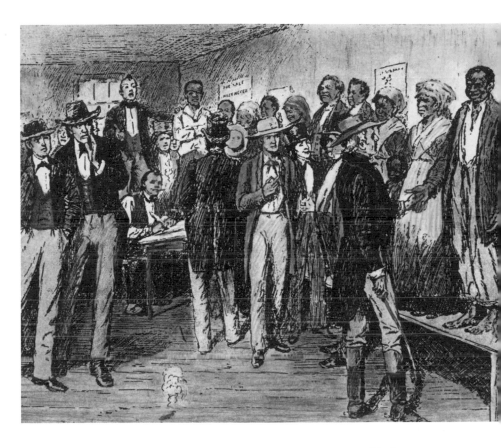

saddened by the sight of men, women, and children being driven along in chains and sold like cattle.

Abraham and Allen sold their cargo and their flatboat, and returned upriver by steamboat. Altogether, the trip took three months. Abraham earned $24, which by law went to his father.

When Abraham returned to Indiana, he began to spend more and more time away from home, often working for the local blacksmith. He spent his free time with friends his age. Abraham gained popularity

Nineteen-year-old Abraham Lincoln (second from left) saw his first slave auction during his visit to New Orleans in 1828.

through storytelling. A crowd never failed to gather whenever Abraham had stories or jokes to share. Abraham liked to entertain his friends by imitating the traveling preachers and politicians of that day.

In 1830, Abraham helped his family move to Macon County, Illinois. Thomas was drawn to Illinois by reports of rich black soil and endless prairies. In addition, rumors had spread that more milk sickness deaths were occurring in southern Indiana. Thomas didn't want to stay and risk having the sickness strike his family again.

After a long, cold trip over rugged terrain, the Lincolns settled about 10 miles (16 km) west of Decatur, Illinois, along the Sangamon River. Abraham spent the first long, cold, prairie winter with his family. In the spring, Abraham felt it was time for him to go out on his own for good.

He knew he didn't want to be a farmer or carpenter like his father, but he didn't know what sort of career to pursue. Abraham agreed to take another boatload

As white settlers moved west, the United States government tried to convince Native Americans who roamed the land to live on reservations. As more white settlers came to Illinois, the government moved the Sauk and Fox Indians across the Mississippi River to a reservation in Iowa. In 1832, a Sauk Indian chief named Black Hawk convinced others to try to move back to their homeland. The U.S. government used military force to put down the uprising, and the conflict became known as the Black Hawk War.

of goods to New Orleans, this time for a man named Denton Offutt. Then Offutt opened a general store in the small community of New Salem, Illinois, and offered Abraham a job. Abraham loved living in New Salem and counted many of the town's 100 residents as his friends. When the store failed in 1832, Abraham did not want to leave. He'd have to find another way to support himself.

Black Hawk, a chief of the Sauk tribe, tried to lead his tribe back into Illinois.

Community leaders in New Salem convinced Abraham Lincoln to run for a seat in the state legislature in 1832. They thought politics might prove to be his calling. But as the election drew nearer, Abraham's attention turned to the Black Hawk War. When the governor of Illinois called upon the militia to end the uprising, Lincoln volunteered to help.

Lincoln joined a group of men from the New Salem area, and they elected him their captain. That day was one of the proudest days of his life.

"[This election was] a success which gave me more pleasure than any I have had since," Lincoln later recalled.

Lincoln served in the militia less than 90 days,

and his men never fought any battles. After his discharge in early July, he still had time to campaign before the election in the fall. It wasn't enough, however, and he lost.

With his military career behind him and no job waiting at the Illinois state capital, Lincoln found another opportunity. A man named William Berry offered to be his partner in a general store in New Salem. Berry knew Lincoln didn't have any money, but he trusted him to pay for his share when he could.

"I believed he was so thoroughly honest, and that impression was so strong in me I accepted his note in payment of the whole," Berry said.

The Berry-Lincoln store sold a variety of goods, from coffee and sugar to hats and fabric. When the business failed, Lincoln again found himself unemployed. He found work at the gristmill, as a farmhand, and once again splitting rails, before he was hired as the town's postmaster.

Lincoln enjoyed his job as postmaster for nearly three years. The position put him in contact with most of the people in the area. It also gave him the

> *William Berry died in 1835 before paying off the failed store's debts. They amounted to approximately $1,100— a huge sum, which Lincoln referred to as the "National Debt." Although Abraham Lincoln had never earned more than a few dollars a month, he resolved to pay off every penny of the debt. It took him 15 years, but he did it.*

The Berry-Lincoln store at Lincoln's New Salem State Historic Site

chance to read all the newspapers that came through his office. He spent as much time as he could spare with his nose in books, newspapers, and anything else he could find.

But the part-time postmaster position paid only $50 a year—not enough to cover Lincoln's expenses. He soon took a second job as assistant to the county surveyor.

Abraham Lincoln didn't know the first thing about surveying, but he knew he could learn. He bought a compass, a chain, and a couple of textbooks on the

The Surveyor,
*by noted
Lincoln artist
Lloyd Ostendorf*

subject, and taught himself the basics of surveying in just six weeks.

The work of a surveyor was difficult. Lincoln often returned home with his clothes dirty and torn from walking through swamps and thick brush. Yet he found the work rewarding. He laid out towns and roads and helped farmers with boundary issues.

Through these two jobs, Abraham Lincoln became well known throughout the county. He earned a reputation as an honest, dependable, and hardworking man. His interest in politics hadn't faded either. In 1834, Lincoln once again ran for election to the Illinois state legislature. This time, the citizens chose Lincoln to represent them.

While working as a legislator, Lincoln began studying law. Lincoln knew he needed to understand the laws of the land in order to be an effective legislator. The people rewarded Abraham Lincoln by reelecting him to three more terms.

During his first term in office, Lincoln met another legislator named Stephen Douglas. Little did the two men know their futures would be closely tied to one another's—both personally and professionally. ℘

In the 1830s, few men attended law school. Instead they found a position "reading law" in the office of a practicing attorney. Since Lincoln was already working as a legislator, he decided to study on his own. After nearly three years of reading and memorizing legal codes and precedents, Lincoln passed his exams. He was admitted to practice law on March 1, 1837.

Chapter 4 FAMILY MAN

❧❧❦❧❧

Although Lincoln possessed a gift for storytelling, he usually felt shy and awkward among eligible young women. But he tried his best, and he eventually won the heart of a young lady named Ann Rutledge. Their romance was short-lived, however. In the summer of 1835, Ann died, probably of typhoid. Years later, Lincoln shared the pain of this loss with a friend. He said:

> *I loved the woman dearly and soundly:*
> *she was a handsome girl—would have*
> *made a good loving wife, I did honestly*
> *and truly love the girl and think often—*
> *often of her now.*

After his first legislative session, Lincoln decided to move to Springfield, Illinois, a town of about 2,000

Abraham Lincoln and his wife, Mary Todd Lincoln, were living proof that opposites attract.

The city of Vandalia became the capital of Illinois in 1820, and remained so for almost 20 years. In 1837, Lincoln was among the state leaders who suggested Springfield as the state's new capital. In 1839, the state government moved to Springfield and has remained there ever since.

people. Springfield had recently been chosen as Illinois' new capital. Having earned his license to practice law, Lincoln accepted a partnership in the Springfield law office of his friend John Stuart.

Aside from the sadness of leaving a community he'd grown to love, Lincoln found the move from New Salem to Springfield to be an easy one. He had few possessions. Everything he owned fit into two saddlebags, which he threw over the back of a horse. In fact, even the horse belonged to someone else. Lincoln borrowed it to get to Springfield.

Twenty-eight-year-old Abraham Lincoln arrived in town with $7 in his pocket. He went to the general store to buy a mattress and other goods he'd need, but soon discovered that he didn't have enough money.

As luck would have it, the owner of the store, Joshua Speed, knew Lincoln by reputation. The kindly man offered to share his room above the store, and Abraham accepted his generosity. It marked the beginning of a lifelong friendship.

Another relationship bloomed for Lincoln in Springfield as well. In 1839, 21-year-old Mary Todd

Joshua Fry Speed (1814-1882), was Lincoln's closest friend in Springfield. The two men shared a room for four years.

moved from Kentucky to live with her sister Elizabeth Edwards in Springfield. The daughter of a wealthy banker, Mary enjoyed the finer things in life. She loved shopping, traveling, dressing up, and going to social events. At one of these social events, Mary met the shy Mr. Lincoln.

Mary found Lincoln interesting, but many men competed for her attention. Among them was Stephen Douglas, whom she dated for a while. Despite his shyness around women, Abraham found the courage to approach Mary at a dance.

"Miss Todd, I want to dance with you in the worst way," he said.

In later years, when Mary would retell this story, she'd laugh and say that's exactly what Abraham did (dance with her in the worst way), hinting that he wasn't a great dancer. Still, Mary saw something she loved in this big, gentle man. While other suitors may have boasted more money and more possessions—the things her family found important—Lincoln didn't even own a house. But Mary saw his potential. She liked the way he listened to her ideas and talked to her about politics and books. In those days, women did not participate in politics, but Abraham never made her feel embarrassed or unladylike for expressing her own opinions.

Elizabeth Edwards, the oldest sister of Mary Todd Lincoln

Despite the objections of her sister, Mary started dating Abraham and soon they became engaged. Their relationship went well until the absentminded Abraham Lincoln forgot about a date he made with her. Angry and hurt, Mary decided to go to the dance on her own.

When Lincoln realized his mistake, he ran to find her. He stopped first at her sister's home but learned Mary wasn't there. He raced to the dance to find Mary in the arms of her old boyfriend, Stephen Douglas.

Having seen Abraham enter the hall, Mary pretended not to notice him. Instead, she flirted with Douglas. Crushed, Lincoln left the dance without talking to her.

Shortly afterward, on January 1, 1841, Abraham asked Mary to release him from their engagement. Mary's family still disapproved, and Abraham thought she deserved more than he would ever be able to offer her. Though her heart was breaking, Mary freed him from their agreement. A depressed Lincoln soon fell ill.

Born in 1818, Mary Todd was nearly 10 years younger than Abraham Lincoln. She also stood more than a foot shorter. Both loved to talk about politics, however, and were attracted to one another despite their differences.

"I am now the most miserable man living," Lincoln wrote to John Stuart. "If what I feel were equally distributed to the whole human family, there would not be one cheerful face on the earth."

Mary suffered, too, but nearly two years passed before friends plotted to get the two back together again. Knowing Mary and Abraham remained miserable without each other, Simeon Francis and his wife invited both of them to their home at the same time.

Mary Todd Lincoln loved to wear enormous hoop skirts, and fresh flowers in her hair.

When they saw each other, Mary and Abraham forgot about the past and rekindled their romance. Soon they became engaged again, but this time, knowing her family wouldn't approve, Mary didn't tell them.

Mary and Abraham set the date for their wedding—November 4, 1842. The day of the ceremony, Mary told Elizabeth she was marrying Abraham Lincoln. While her sister flew into a rage, Mary stood her ground. Meanwhile, Abraham had met Elizabeth's husband, Ninian, on the street and shared the news. Ninian quickly realized the wedding plans were set and would go on with or without the approval of Mary's family. He convinced Elizabeth to open their home for the ceremony that evening.

About 30 close friends gathered for the simple ceremony. Neither the bride's nor the groom's parents were present. Abraham gave Mary a gold wedding ring that he bought in Springfield. The words "Love is Eternal" were engraved inside the band.

Since Lincoln couldn't afford to take Mary on a honeymoon, the couple moved right into a boardinghouse called the Globe Tavern. The cost of their meals and an 8-foot by 14-foot (2.4-m by 4-m) room at the Globe was $4 a month.

Abraham and Mary's first son was born on August 1, 1843, and was named Robert Todd in honor of Mary's father. Lincoln knew the boardinghouse would be too noisy and uncomfortable for his growing family, so they moved out and began renting a small cottage. A few months later, Lincoln was able to purchase a larger home with financial help from

The Lincolns purchased this house in Springfield for $1,500 in 1844. It was the only home they ever owned.

Mary's father. The new house, at the corner of Eighth and Jackson streets, would remain their home for the next 17 years.

Married life proved to be an adjustment for Mary. She was used to having servants do most of the housework. Now the burden of keeping a comfortable home fell completely on her shoulders. She didn't complain, however, because she loved her husband and their newborn son, Robert.

On March 10, 1846, Abraham and Mary welcomed a second son to the family. His name was Edward Baker, but he was always known as "Eddie."

By this time, Lincoln had opened his own law office just a few blocks from home, and hired William Herndon as his junior partner. Lincoln's business continued to grow. Soon he was able to pay off the last of his debts from the Berry-Lincoln store in New Salem.

In the fall of 1846, Lincoln was elected to the U.S. House of Representatives in Washington, D.C. But after one two year term, he returned to Springfield, eager to move on with his life and spend more time with his family.

Then disaster struck. In December 1849, little Eddie became very ill, most likely with tuberculosis. Eddie died on February 1, 1850. He was not quite 4 years old. Abraham and Mary were devastated. Mary shut herself in her room to grieve, while Abraham buried himself in his work.

But more children were soon to follow. William Wallace, called "Willie," was born in December of that same year, followed by Thomas, called "Tad," in April 1853. And so, life went on. ✑

5 BATTLING AGAINST DOUGLAS

With his career as a legislator behind him, Lincoln settled comfortably into his law practice full time. Because many lawyers lived in Springfield, competition for business proved fierce. Lawyers had to charge lower fees in order to attract clients. Yet Lincoln's practice thrived. His reputation as an honest, hard-working man brought him lots of clients, though it didn't make him terribly rich.

Lincoln may have been content to spend the rest of his life as a Springfield lawyer had not the issue of slavery aroused his anger. In the 1850s, the country was divided on the question of whether slavery should be abolished or allowed to expand as the United States grew westward. As each new state joined the Union, arguments arose over whether or

For most of his life, Abraham Lincoln was clean-shaven, as shown in this portrait by George Peter Alexander Healy.

not slavery should be allowed there. The Missouri Compromise of 1820 had settled the issue for a time by defining the future boundary between slave and free states in the western territories of the United States.

In 1854, Lincoln faced off against a familiar opponent—Stephen Douglas, Mary's former boyfriend. Now a powerful U.S. senator, Douglas had introduced a bill known as the Kansas-Nebraska Act, supporting the idea that states should be allowed to decide for themselves whether they would come into the Union slave or free. Senator Douglas' idea, known as "popular sovereignty," brought strong reactions from people both for and against slavery.

Established in 1820, the Missouri Compromise kept the balance between the number of free states and slave states in the Union. Congress admitted Missouri as a slave state on the condition that no other slave states could be formed from territory north of the 36 degrees 30 minutes north latitude line, Missouri's southern border. At the same time, Maine was admitted as a new free state, keeping the balance between slave and free states.

Since both Kansas and Nebraska fell north of the line established by the Missouri Compromise, these territories should have been off-limits to slavery. Senator Douglas' idea could not be put into effect unless the Missouri Compromise was overturned.

Lincoln strongly opposed the spread of slavery

Stephen Arnold Douglas (1813-1861) was nicknamed "The Little Giant" by the press. Although he was only 5 feet 4 inches (163 cm) tall, Douglas had a booming voice and an aggressive manner

into these and future territories of the United States. When Lincoln first heard news that the Missouri Compromise was about to be repealed, he was stunned. It was his anger regarding this issue that drew him back into politics.

As Douglas traveled around Illinois trying to gain support for his ideas about the slavery issue, Lincoln followed him and shared the opposite side of the issue. In Peoria, Illinois, on October 16, 1854, Abraham Lincoln spoke passionately against the spread of slavery by saying:

I think, and shall try to show, that it is wrong; wrong in its direct effect, letting slavery into Kansas and Nebraska—and wrong in prospective principle, allowing it to spread to every other part of the wide world, where men can be found inclined to take it. ... Before proceeding, let me say I think I have no prejudice against the Southern people. They are just what we would be in their situation. If slavery did not now exist amongst them, they would not introduce it. If it did now exist amongst us, we should not instantly give it up. ... Doubtless there are individuals, on both sides, who would not hold slaves under any circumstances; and others who would gladly introduce slavery anew, if it were out of existence.

Lincoln argued that slavery went against the very principle upon which the country was originally founded—freedom. The Declaration of Independence stated each citizen's right to be free, yet some Americans held others in chains.

But Lincoln also understood how difficult getting rid of slavery would be. By the 1850s, the Southern economy depended upon slave labor to thrive. And the idea of freeing all the slaves presented other problems, too. What would become of them after they were freed? Most were uneducated and knew no other lifestyle. Where would they go? What kinds of jobs could they find? While many

people in the North favored the freeing of slaves, would these people welcome the newly freed blacks into their communities, their churches, and their workplaces?

Although a great majority of Southerners owned no slaves at all, most still believed that slavery was right and proper.

Lincoln didn't pretend to have all the answers, but he felt strongly on one point: The Missouri Compromise should stand, and if it did, he believed slavery would die out eventually on its own.

Lincoln did whatever he could to oppose Douglas and his supporters. In 1858, when he accepted the nomination to run against Douglas for a seat in the U.S. Senate, Lincoln said:

A house divided against itself cannot stand. I believe this government cannot endure, permanently half slave and half free. I do not expect the Union to be dissolved—I do not expect the house to fall—but I do expect it will cease to be divided. It will become all one thing, or all the other.

In order to get his message out to the public without confusion, Lincoln challenged Douglas to a series of formal political debates. The debates were held in the fall of 1858, at seven sites throughout Illinois—one in each of the seven congressional districts.

The Lincoln-Douglas debates began in Ottawa, Illinois, on August 21, and ended on October 15 in the town of Alton. At each site, great crowds gathered to hear the men talk. People came for hundreds of miles to hear the debate. In fact, the Lincoln-Douglas debates drew the attention of the entire nation. The debates helped Americans decide how they really felt about slavery.

In his speeches, Lincoln pointed to the basic truth of the Declaration of Independence—the truth of human equality. America was built upon the idea that all men are created equal. And because all individuals have the same rights by nature, one group of people cannot rightfully enslave another.

Although Abraham Lincoln was relatively unknown at the beginning of the debates, he soon became a

household name. The debates put Lincoln in the national spotlight. Stephen Douglas eventually won the Senate race, but by only a few votes.

Political debates were a source of great entertainment in the mid-1800s.

In May 1860, the Republican Party nominated Abraham Lincoln to be its candidate in the presidential election. Meanwhile, the Democratic party had split in two. Northern Democrats nominated Stephen Douglas, while Southern, pro-slavery

Democrats chose John Breckinridge. A fourth candidate, John Bell, was nominated by the Constitutional Union party.

Though he personally hated slavery, Lincoln's main concern was the preservation of the Union. He said he didn't intend to end slavery in the South at the risk of dividing the country.

Abraham Lincoln was the first man born outside the 13 original colonies to be elected president.

Many Southerners thought Lincoln was lying. They warned that if he were elected president, the nation would literally be divided. The Southern states would leave the Union and form their own country.

Abraham Lincoln won the election with a huge

ABRAHAM LINCOLN,

REPUBLICAN CANDIDATE FOR PRESIDENT OF THE UNITED STATES.

percentage of the electoral vote, even though he received less than 40 percent of the popular vote. More than 2.8 million votes were cast against Lincoln, but these votes were divided among the other three candidates. Lincoln himself earned more than 1.8 million votes from the American people, and was named the next president.

On November 6, 1860, Lincoln waited anxiously as results of the election dribbled in at the telegraph office in Springfield. Close friends joined him to offer their support, and a crowd gathered outside, hoping for good news for their candidate.

When the results clearly showed that Lincoln was the new president of the United States, his friends ran outside to share the news with the crowd. Abraham just wanted to go home and tell his wife.

"I guess I'll go down and tell Mary about it," Abraham said to a friend.

After rushing home, he couldn't contain himself.

"Mary, Mary! We are elected!" he exclaimed.

> *The electoral college is a group of people who elect the U.S. president. Each state is given a certain number of electoral votes, equal to the number of its U.S. senators (two from each state) plus the number of its U.S. representatives (determined by the size of each state's population). The candidate who receives the most votes from the people in a state is awarded that state's electoral votes. For example, a state may have more than 50 electoral votes, while another state may have only three.*

Chapter

6 MR. PRESIDENT

༙

To many people in the South, Abraham Lincoln's victory in the 1860 presidential election seemed like a declaration of war against them. Even though Lincoln promised not to force his views on the country, people knew he hated slavery. While he didn't suggest abolishing slavery, he did not want it to spread into other states. He hoped that by limiting slavery's growth, eventually it would die out altogether. Southern plantation owners who relied on slave labor didn't believe the new president's promise, and vowed to fight for their way of life.

Even before Lincoln took office, Southern states began seceding from the Union. South Carolina was the first to leave, in December 1860. One after another, 11 Southern states seceded from the Union, a move

The President and Mrs. Lincoln greet Union generals, Cabinet members, and other guests at a grand White House reception.

Lincoln refused to accept. On February 4, 1861, representatives from these 11 states met and formed their own government. They elected Jefferson Davis as president, and Alexander Stephens as vice president, of the Confederate States of America. The following May, Richmond, Virginia, was chosen as the Confederate capital.

Although the president still held out hope that the differences between North and South could be resolved, that hope was shattered on April 12, 1861, when Confederate soldiers fired on a U.S. military

April 12, 1861: Confederate cannons fired on Fort Sumter at Charleston Harbor, South Carolina.

post in the harbor at Charleston, South Carolina. The bloodiest war in American history—the U.S. Civil War—had begun. Abraham Lincoln would be leading a nation at war.

When the Lincolns arrived at the White House, or Executive Mansion, on March 4, 1861, they found broken furniture, worn carpets, torn draperies, and a basement infested with rats. Mary felt strongly that this home did not fit the image the president of the United States should show the world.

When Congress approved a budget of $20,000 for White House improvements, Mary quickly went to work turning the home into one the country could be proud of. When she completed her work, however, Mary found she'd spent about $6,700 more than budgeted. Lincoln couldn't believe it.

In Lincoln's day, the White House was a public building. Anyone could wander in at any time of the day or night. The first floor was completely open to the public, as was much of the second floor. The only rooms that remained off-limits were the family quarters on the second floor.

"It would stink in the nostrils of the American people to have it said that the President of the United States had approved a bill overrunning an appropriation of $20,000 for *flub dubs* for this damned old house, when the soldiers cannot have blankets," he exclaimed.

Though Lincoln vowed to pay back the extra cost himself, he couldn't scrape up the money. Quietly, Congress took care of the bills to avoid stirring up the public.

The public certainly wasn't afraid to let Lincoln

know its thoughts. Each day, the new president received around 250 letters. A staff of three young men was needed to sort and distribute this mail. Many letters could be passed on to Cabinet members and others who could answer the questions they contained. The staff members threw away death threats, but letters requiring the president's attention always got a personal response from Lincoln himself.

People also lined up every day to see President Lincoln in person. Some came with important business. Others just wished to shake his hand. Lincoln made sure no one was turned away. It wasn't unusual to see the line from his second-floor office stretching down the stairs and to the front door.

Lincoln also had other work to accomplish and meetings to attend. Friends worried the president didn't get enough time away from his desk to stay healthy. Still, Lincoln felt that this was the life he'd chosen when he ran for president.

"They [the citizens] do not want much, and they get very little," he told his concerned friends. "I know how I would feel in their place."

Abraham and Mary Lincoln did find time for fun, however. On February 5, 1862, the Lincolns invited 500 guests to a reception to show off the newly remodeled White House.

The Lincolns nearly canceled the party when Willie and Tad fell

> *Tad and Willie Lincoln, ages 8 and 10, had a great time in their new home. The two boys terrorized the White House staff and created frequent disturbances in the Executive Mansion. They burst into solemn Cabinet meetings, brought goats and other pets into the White House, sold food to visitors in the lobby, and once tried to fire a cannon from the roof of the White House.*

Abraham and Mary Lincoln in the White House with sons Robert and Tad. A portrait of Willie Lincoln hangs on the wall.

ill, but a doctor assured them the boys would be fine. Still, the caring parents sneaked up to the family's quarters during the party to check on them.

During the next two weeks, Tad remained sick, and Willie grew worse. Tad eventually recovered, but

11-year-old Willie died on February 20, 1862. The Lincolns were devastated. Abraham and Mary had already lost their son Eddie in Springfield, back in 1850. Now the death of Willie seemed too much to bear.

Mary couldn't bring herself to attend Willie's funeral or take care of young Tad, who suffered from nightmares after his brother's death. Instead, she took to her bed. As his wife slipped further into despair, Lincoln hired a nurse to help care for her.

Also grieving, the president clung to his work. It had been almost a year since the Confederate soldiers had first fired on Fort Sumter and had begun the Civil War. As the fighting continued, Lincoln found sleeping difficult. He sometimes got so wrapped up in his work, he'd forget to eat. The pain left by Willie's death and the strain of trying to end the Civil War took its toll on Lincoln's body. The president looked exhausted and extremely thin—almost skeletal.

Lincoln put in long days. He'd go to his office and begin working even before breakfast. After downing an egg and some coffee, he'd again head

>
>
> *Mary Lincoln's mental health proved fragile, and no one knew how to deal with it in those days. Some even took advantage of her condition. These people convinced Mary that it was possible to contact Willie from beyond the grave, which she tried to do at least eight different times. The president constantly worried about his wife while he continued with the difficult work of governing the nation.*

The stress of the war is visible on Lincoln's face in this 1862 photo by Mathew Brady.

back to his office. If he remembered to stop for lunch, he usually ate just an apple and drank a glass of milk before returning to business. Sometimes he'd give himself a break and go for a carriage ride in the afternoon, but most often he'd just continue working late into the night, unless he was expected to attend a reception or other official function.

At the very end of his day, Lincoln usually walked across the White House lawn to the War Department. Here he'd read any official news from the front lines of the war. After reading about the death and destruction on the battlefields, it was no wonder sleep would not come to him.

The president's long days were difficult for Mary, too, though she understood the difficulties her husband faced.

"I consider myself fortunate, if at eleven o'clock, I once more find myself, in my pleasant room and very especially, if my tired and weary Husband is there, waiting in the lounge to receive me," the first lady said.

Abraham Lincoln sometimes read to his Cabinet from the works of the great humorists. He'd often read until he laughed so hard the tears streamed down his face. Lincoln explained that he needed these times of laughter to be able to deal with all the death and destruction caused by the Civil War.

In the summer of 1862, the Lincolns took a much-needed vacation. They stayed in a cottage just north of Washington, D.C. With the Civil War still raging, Lincoln made daily trips back to the White House to attend to business. It has been rumored that on one of these journeys, a bullet pierced the president's hat. Whether the shot was fired by accident or by a potential assassin was never determined.

7 CONVICTION AND CONTROVERSY

∽⁓∾

As president, Abraham Lincoln was hated in the South. In fact, he wasn't wildly popular in the North either. During the Civil War, many people throughout the country feared he wasn't doing the right thing. Some people pushed for the abolition of slavery. Others just wanted the conflict to end and the nation to be reunited. Lincoln didn't bow to pressure from anyone. Despite much criticism, he never shied away from making decisions he felt were right.

Many on both sides of the battle believed the Civil War would end quickly. Men in the North answered Lincoln's call to enlist in the Army, thinking one big battle would crush the Confederate states and bring the war to an end. When Union forces were defeated in the first Battle of Bull Run on July 21, 1861, Northerners were faced with the fact that the Southern states planned to put up a strong fight.

The North had every advantage: superior manpower, factories for making guns and ammunition, control of the railroads, and a navy of ships to block supplies from reaching Southern ports.

The South, however, fought with great passion and made full use of its one significant advantage: talented military leadership.

In November 1862, Lincoln was so frustrated by General George McClellan's failure to follow up on his victory at the Battle of Antietam, that he is said to have told him, "If you don't want to use the army, I should like to borrow it for a while." Lincoln then dismissed McClellan and appointed General Ambrose E. Burnside general-in-chief in his place.

Both Jefferson Davis, president of the Confederacy, and his top military adviser, General Robert E. Lee, were experienced, professional soldiers. Union commanders, in contrast, proved excellent at training their troops, but slow to put them to use.

As the war dragged on, Lincoln struggled to find a commander capable of leading the Union forces to victory. He appointed and fired a series of generals. In less than one year, five different men served as general-in-chief of the Union Army.

At first, since Lincoln himself was not a military man, he didn't feel right telling his generals what to do. Then Edward Bates, Lincoln's attorney general, told the president that it was his duty to "command the commanders."

"The nation requires it," Bates said, "and history will hold you responsible."

Lincoln began to study military strategy, once again teaching himself through books he collected on the subject. Lincoln studied very hard, and soon took charge of the daily business of the war.

In an attempt to bring the country back together, Lincoln issued the Emancipation Proclamation. It became one of the most controversial decisions of his presidency.

The Battle of Antietam in Maryland, on September 17, 1862, remains the bloodiest day in U.S. military history. There were nearly 23,000 casualties.

> The Emancipation
> Proclamation was a
> wartime measure, and
> had a limited effect.
> The 13th Amendment
> to the Constitution,
> adopted in December
> 1865, permanently
> abolished slavery
> throughout the
> United States.

After a Union victory in September 1862 at the Battle of Antietam, Maryland, the president announced his plan to free all the slaves in states that continued to rebel against the Union. Lincoln gave the Confederate states until January 1, 1863, to rejoin the Union and avoid this consequence.

Holding true to his word, Lincoln put into effect the official Emancipation Proclamation on January 1, 1863. While federal officials really had no power to go into the Confederate states and enforce Lincoln's proclamation, the words raised the Union cause in the eyes of foreign countries. It also encouraged Northern abolitionists who had been begging the president all along to end slavery.

The Union Army pressed on in 1863 and continued to score important victories.

On July 1-3, 1863, Union troops led by General George G. Meade clashed with the Confederate forces of General Robert E. Lee in a fierce and bloody three-day battle around a little town called Gettysburg, Pennsylvania. When the Battle of Gettysburg was over, more than 50,000 soldiers were dead, wounded, or missing. Lee's battered

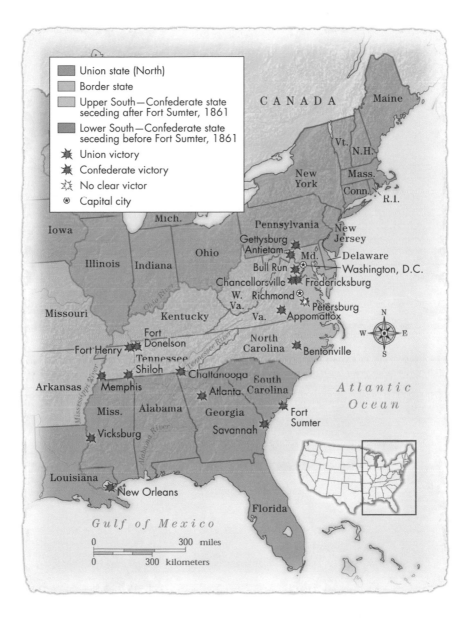

Union state (North)

Border state

Upper South—Confederate state seceding after Fort Sumter, 1861

Lower South—Confederate state seceding before Fort Sumter, 1861

Union victory

Confederate victory

No clear victor

Capital city

Confederate Army retreated to Virginia in defeat.

Around the same time, General Ulysses S. Grant captured the Confederacy's last stronghold on the

Most battles of the Civil War were fought in the South.

73

Mississippi River. Grant and his Army of the West had finally forced the surrender of Vicksburg, Mississippi, after a six-week siege.

Lincoln again held out hope that the end of the war was close at hand. In August 1863, he began to share his ideas for Reconstruction—the work of rebuilding the South after the war and bringing the rebel states back into the Union. President Lincoln hoped the Southern states would adopt emancipation and establish "some practical system by which the two races could gradually [outgrow] their old relation to each other, and both come out better prepared for the new. Education for young blacks should be included in the plan."

Plans also were made to dedicate a cemetery on the site of the Gettysburg battle. There, on November 19, 1863, Edward Everett, one of the greatest speakers of his day, rose to address the crowd. Although Everett talked for nearly two hours, it would be President Lincoln's brief, yet heartfelt, two-minute speech that would forever be remembered.

In fewer than 300 words, Lincoln expressed what he had lately come to see as the larger meaning of the war. He explained that, as long as slavery was allowed, the United States could never be the free and democratic country it was meant to be. He said:

Four score and seven years ago our fathers brought forth on this continent, a new nation, conceived in liberty, and dedicated to the proposition that all men are created equal. Now we are engaged in a great civil war, testing whether that nation, or any nation so conceived and so dedicated, can long endure. We are met on a great battlefield of that war. We have come to dedicate a portion of that field, as a final resting place for those who here gave their lives that that nation might live.

At the time, many people—including Lincoln himself—considered his short speech at Gettysburg a failure.

The president continued, saying the words spoken at this dedication would fade from memory long before the sacrifices made by the soldiers who fought at Gettysburg. He urged those listening to honor those sacrifices by rallying to the Union cause, saying:

> *It is for us the living, rather, to be dedicated here to the unfinished work which they who fought here have thus far so nobly advanced. It is rather for us to be here dedicated to the great task remaining before us—that from these honored dead we take increased devotion to that cause for which they gave the last full measure of devotion—that we here highly resolve that these dead shall not have died in vain—that this nation, under God, shall have a new birth of freedom—and that government of the people, by the people, for the people, shall not perish from the earth.*

Although Union victories earlier that year had seemed to promise peace on the horizon, the war waged on. Lincoln prepared himself for the fact he'd likely lose his bid for reelection in 1864.

In March 1864, Lincoln had placed General Grant in command of all the Union armies. While Lincoln stood by his decision, many nicknamed the general "the butcher" because of all the casualties the Army suffered. The public was tired of war and death, and some were in favor of peace at any cost.

The tide of the war turned, however, beginning

in late summer of 1864. Admiral David Farragut claimed victory in the Battle of Mobile Bay on August 5. Less than a month later, General William T. Sherman's troops captured Atlanta, Georgia. In November, with 62,000 men, Sherman began his "march to the sea." By December 21, the Union Army had cut a 60-mile (96-km) wide path of destruction all the way from Atlanta to Savannah, Georgia. In a telegraph, Sherman offered the city of Savannah to President Lincoln as a Christmas present.

General Sherman vowed to "make Georgia howl." His troops destroyed everything in their path.

By the time the election rolled around, citizens rallied to support the president. Lincoln earned a clear victory against his opponent, the same George McClellan he had dismissed from military duty two years earlier.

In his second inaugural address, Lincoln declared the war God's punishment for the sin of slavery.

As Lincoln took the oath of office for the second time, Americans knew the end of the war was in sight. Barely a month later, on April 9, 1865, Confederate General Robert E. Lee surrendered to General Grant at Appomattox Court House, Virginia. When the news reached Washington, D.C., the next day, a joyous crowd began gathering outside the White House.

"The bands played, the howitzers belched forth their thunder, and the people cheered," read a report in the *National Intelligencer* newspaper. The crowd called out for the president to appear. Finally Lincoln came out, addressed the crowd in a relaxed and humorous way, and requested that the band play "Dixie" for him.

Despite his humor, Lincoln knew much work lay ahead for the wounded country. In an official speech on April 11, the president spoke to the public about Reconstruction. It seemed that everyone had a different idea regarding how to rebuild the Southern states and bring them back into the Union. Lincoln welcomed input on this difficult issue. He was confident the country could tackle the problem together—one day at a time.

"The pilots on our Western rivers steer from point to point as they call it—setting the course of the boat no farther than they can see; and that is all I propose to myself in this great problem," Lincoln explained. ᴖ

8 ASSASSINATION

❧

From the start of his presidency, Abraham Lincoln received hate mail. Some letter writers went so far as to threaten the new president's life. The threats and the worry they caused Mary worsened the migraines she'd suffered with most of her life.

In Lincoln's day, presidents didn't have Secret Service agents protecting them. It hadn't seemed necessary. But as the death threats continued to arrive at the White House, Lincoln's advisers insisted on taking precautions. Armed bodyguards were hired to protect the president, and cavalry officers escorted his private carriage. Lincoln complained about this protection, but he put up with it—even the soldiers camped on the White House lawn.

At the time, many people found the theater friv-

Howard Pyle painted President Lincoln in his office at the White House for his book, The American Spirit.

olous or even sinful, but Lincoln loved it. He often attended productions at Ford's Theatre with Mary at his side. It was at Ford's Theatre that Lincoln saw performances by a popular actor named John Wilkes Booth.

A handsome 26-year-old, Booth was arguably one of the most popular stage actors of his day. Still, Booth chose to take a break from his career during the Civil War and serve as a Confederate spy.

John Wilkes Booth saw President Lincoln as an evil tyrant. The actor believed in the Confederate cause and firmly supported slavery. He even helped hatch a kidnapping plot against the president during the war. Booth had suggested kidnapping Lincoln in an effort to secure the release of Confederate prisoners of war.

In February 1861, a scheme to assassinate Lincoln on a train was uncovered. To avoid the threat, the president chose to take an earlier train. While he did change his schedule on this particular occasion, Lincoln generally refused to let threats disrupt his life or make him live in fear.

Booth wanted to kidnap the president at the theater, a place he knew well, but those conspiring with Booth thought it would be too difficult and risky. With the surrender at Appomattox Court House, the Civil War was nearing its end and the kidnapping plot was scratched.

Yet Booth's hatred for Abraham Lincoln grew.

John Wilkes Booth (1838-1865), Lincoln's assassin

When the president gave a speech from the White House on April 11, Booth and some of his friends were there. In this, his last public speech, Lincoln talked about his plans for the country and added that he believed African-Americans should have the right to vote. This enraged Booth and furthered his belief that Lincoln was a tyrant who dictated his beliefs to the people.

Earlier that day, Lincoln had told a friend about a dream he'd recently had. He'd dreamt of his own death. Little did the president know that John Wilkes Booth was dreaming of the same thing.

Booth seized the opportunity to put his plan into action April 14. Booth heard that Lincoln had reserved seats in the presidential box at Ford's Theatre for a production of the play *Our American Cousin*. As an actor who'd worked in this theater, Booth knew his way around. He gave up the idea of kidnapping Lincoln and decided instead to kill him. Booth figured he could get close enough to Lincoln in his reserved box to kill him and still be able to escape.

Abraham Lincoln often had premonitions. After the election of 1860, he saw two images of himself in a mirror, one paler than the other. Mary later believed this was a sign that Abraham would be elected president twice, but would die before he finished his second term in office.

The assassination of the president was one of three related murders to be attempted that evening. All were to happen at about the same time so word wouldn't get out and cause any of the three intended targets to change their plans. Along with Lincoln, Vice President Andrew Johnson and Secretary of State William Seward were targeted for death. The would-be assassin of Johnson got cold feet and made no attempt, but Seward was stabbed in his bed. Although seriously injured, Seward would survive.

A program for the performance the night of Lincoln's assassination

Before going to the theater that evening, President Lincoln spent part of the day with his wife. When the two took a carriage ride together, Mary noticed how cheerful her husband seemed. The Civil War was at its end, and Lincoln was able to look toward the future with hope.

That evening at the theater, Abraham and Mary Lincoln arrived with their friends Major Henry Rathbone and his fiancée, Clara Harris. A guard also attended with the small group, but during the performance, he may have sat in an open seat instead of in the presidential box.

A beautiful American flag bunting decorated the front of the president's box. As Lincoln took his seat, the orchestra welcomed him with a rousing version of "Hail to the Chief."

During the play's third act,

the people in the large audience roared with laughter. Using the noise to cover the sound of his gun firing, Booth raised the weapon and aimed at the back of the president's head. Mary, who was holding Abraham's hand at the time, noticed the president slumped in his seat. She began to scream.

For some unknown reason, Booth dropped the gun and attacked Major Rathbone with a knife. As he tried to make his escape, Booth caught one of his spurs on the bunting on the front of the president's box. As he jumped to the stage, the assassin broke a bone in his ankle. He made his way out the exit in the back of the theater, but he knew he'd need medical attention.

While this drama was playing out in the president's box, the audience realized what had happened. Panic spread as the frightened people stampeded toward the exits.

A surgeon in the audience hurried to aid the president, who had quit breathing and no longer had a pulse. The doctor resuscitated Lincoln, but soon realized—after sweeping his hand through the president's hair—how badly he had been hurt. As three more doctors came to the president's box, they too could see that Lincoln's wound was fatal.

Believing the president wouldn't live long enough to make it back to the White House, a group of soldiers carried him to a boarding house across

the street. The house's owner offered a bed where the president could spend his final hours. Since Lincoln's body was too long for the bed, he was laid diagonally across it.

More than 100 visitors came to Lincoln's bedside to weep and say goodbye. Lincoln's son Robert joined Mary at his side, but Tad, too young to deal with the horrible tragedy, stayed at the White House.

Overwhelmed, Mary was led to another room as the president's breathing grew more labored. At 7:22 A.M., April 15, 1865, Abraham Lincoln died. His doctors delivered the news to an already grieving Mary.

Family members and prominent Union leaders gathered around the deathbed of Abraham Lincoln. Vice President Andrew Johnson (front left) would become president.

"It is all over!" one of the doctors cried. "The President is no more!"

Outside the White House, a crowd of African-Americans gathered to mourn the loss of the president. The Civil War was over, and they'd gained their

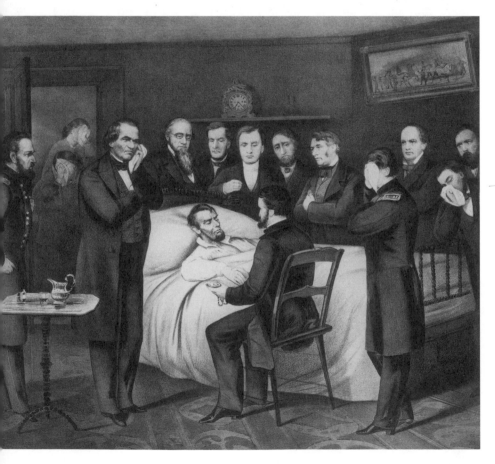

freedom, but what would happen to them now that their champion was gone? Lincoln's death was a shock to many. No American president had ever been killed by an assassin.

The president's body was placed in a casket in the White House. Thousands of people filed past his coffin to pay their respects. Overcome with grief, Mary stayed away from the funeral events and mourned in private.

Mary Todd Lincoln never recovered from her husband's death. For the rest of her life, she dressed in full mourning costume, wearing heavy black crepe dresses and a black bonnet with a black veil. She never went to the theater again.

On April 21, at Mary's direction, the body of Abraham Lincoln was put on a train headed for Illinois. The remains of Willie Lincoln were removed from a temporary tomb in Georgetown and placed on the funeral train as well. All along the way, mourners gathered to say goodbye to the president. On May 4, the caskets arrived in Springfield and were buried at Oak Ridge Cemetery.

Immediately after the president's death, a manhunt began for the murderer and his accomplices. In the meantime, several Southerners helped Booth in his escape toward Virginia. As he hid from authorities, Booth was shocked to learn from the newspapers that people saw him as a villain, not the hero he expected to be.

A dying John Wilkes Booth was dragged from the burning barn in which he had been hiding.

While hiding in a barn in the Virginia countryside, Booth's luck ran out. On April 26, soldiers tried to flush the assassin out by setting the barn ablaze. Though Secretary of War Edwin M. Stanton had made it clear he wanted Booth brought back alive, one of the soldiers fired a shot that hit Booth in the neck, severing his spine.

The manhunt continued until all Booth's conspirators were brought to justice. On May 9, eight people, including one woman, were brought before a military court. Their trial lasted from May 10 through June 29. Because they were tried in a military court rather than a regular civil court, the defendants' rights were limited. They weren't allowed to testify or even to speak during the trial. Four of the defendants—George Atzerodt, David Herold, Lewis Powell, and Mary Surratt—were sentenced to hang.

The public was shocked at the prospect of a woman being hanged. In fact, until the moment of her death, many believed a last-minute pardon would save her. It never did. On July 7, those sentenced to death received their penalties. ॐ

9 LEGACY

Chapter

⧸⧸✕⧹⧹

Despite Lincoln's early death, his legacy lives on. In 1922, work was completed on the Lincoln Memorial in Washington, D.C. The memorial was built to resemble the Parthenon, a famous temple in Greece. Ancient Greece was the home of the first democratic government.

Like the Parthenon, the Lincoln Memorial is surrounded by a colonnade—or a series of columns supporting a roof. The memorial has a total of 36 columns, one for each state in the newly reunited Union at the time of Lincoln's death. The name of each state appears above a column.

The Lincoln Memorial has become a symbol of courage and freedom. It has been the site of some of the most memorable events in American history,

The sculpture by Daniel Chester French of a seated Abraham Lincoln is the centerpiece of the Lincoln Memorial in Washington, D.C.

Emancipation Proclamation: The greatest work of a great American president

including perhaps the most famous speech about freedom given since the days of the Civil War. During the push for civil rights for African-Americans in the 1960s, the Reverend Martin Luther King Jr. chose the Lincoln Memorial as the site for his famous "I Have a Dream" speech.

To many, Abraham Lincoln still represents the

American Dream. He went from a log cabin to the White House. He showed that people, regardless of their backgrounds, can make a difference in the world if they are willing to stand up for their beliefs.

As president during the American Civil War, Lincoln was the most unpopular president the nation had ever known. He was called an amateur, a hick, and a stupid baboon. Yet Lincoln possessed the perfect combination of qualities necessary for great leadership: honesty, compassion, courage, and a good sense of right and wrong. He respected hard work, and he believed in the importance of education and learning. Above all, Abraham Lincoln was ambitious. He never stopped working to improve himself and the world around him.

Several years after the war, abolitionist writer and former slave Frederick Douglass summed up the greatness of the 16th president, saying:

> *His greatest mission was to accomplish two things: first, to save his country from dismemberment and ruin; and, second, to free his country from the great crime of slavery. ... Infinite wisdom has seldom sent any man into the world better fitted for his mission than Abraham Lincoln.*

LINCOLN'S LIFE

1818

Lincoln's mother, Nancy, dies of milk sickness

1816

The Lincoln family moves to Indiana

1819

Lincoln's father, Thomas, marries Sarah Bush Johnston

1809

Born February 12 near present-day Hodgenville, Kentucky

1810

1809

Louis Braille of France, inventor of a writing system for the blind, is born

1814-1815

European states meet in Vienna, Austria, to redraw national borders after the conclusion of the Napoleonic Wars

1821

Central American countries gain independence from Spain

WORLD EVENTS

1828

Travels by flatboat
to New Orleans;
sees his first slave
auction

1830

The Lincoln
family moves
to Illinois

1832

Runs for a seat in
the state legislature
but is defeated;
serves as a militia
captain in the Black
Hawk War

1830

1829

The first practical
sewing machine is
invented by French
tailor Barthélemy
Thimonnier

1833

Great Britain
abolishes slavery

LINCOLN'S LIFE

1843
First son, Robert
Todd Lincoln, is
born August 1

1842
Marries
Mary Todd
November 4

1834
Runs for a seat in
the state legislature
and is elected

1846
Son Edward
is born
March 10

1835

1836
Texans defeat
Mexican troops at San
Jacinto after a deadly
battle at the Alamo

1840
Auguste Rodin,
famous sculptor
of *The Thinker*,
is born

1846
Irish potato
famine reaches
its worst

WORLD EVENTS

1847

Takes seat in the U.S. House of Representatives

1850

Son Eddie dies February 1; son William is born December 21

1853

Son Thomas "Tad" is born April 4

1850

1848

The Communist Manifesto by German writer Karl Marx is widely distributed

1851

Ariel and Umbriel, moons of Uranus, are discovered by William Lassell

LINCOLN'S LIFE

1858

Competes in a
series of Illinois
debates against
Stephen Douglas

1860

Elected president
in November;
Southern states
begin to secede
in December

1861

Sworn in as president
March 4; Civil War
begins April 12 when
Confederate soldiers
fire on Fort Sumter

1860

1858

English scientist
Charles Darwin
presents his theory
of evolution

1860

Austrian composer
Gustav Mahler is born
in Kalischt (now
in Austria)

WORLD EVENTS

1862

Son Willie dies February 20 at the White House

1863

Issues the Emancipation Proclamation January 1; delivers the Gettysburg Address November 19

1865

Lee surrenders to Grant at Appomattox Court House April 9; Lincoln is shot by John Wilkes Booth April 14, and dies the next day

1865

1862

Victor Hugo publishes *Les Misérables*

1863

Construction begins on the first transcontinental railroad in Sacramento, California

1865

Lewis Carroll writes *Alice's Adventures in Wonderland*

DATE OF BIRTH: February 12, 1809

BIRTHPLACE: Near present-day
Hodgenville, Kentucky

FATHER: Thomas Lincoln
(1778-1851)

MOTHER: Nancy Hanks Lincoln
(1784-1818)

STEPMOTHER: Sarah Bush Johnston
(1788-1869)

SPOUSE: Mary Todd Lincoln
(1818-1882)

DATE OF
MARRIAGE: November 4, 1842

CHILDREN: Robert (1843-1926)
Edward (1846-1850)
William (1850-1862)
Thomas (1853-1871)

DATE OF DEATH: April 15, 1865

PLACE OF BURIAL: Springfield, Illinois

In the Library

Ashabranner, Brent K., and Jennifer Ashabranner. *A Memorial for Mr. Lincoln*. New York: Putnam, 1992.

Bracken, Thomas. *Abraham Lincoln*. Philadelphia: Chelsea House Publishers, 1998.

Burgan, Michael. *The Gettysburg Address*. Minneapolis: Compass Point Books, 2006.

Cothran, Helen. *Abraham Lincoln*. San Diego: Greenhaven Press, 2002.

Marrin, Albert. *Commander in Chief: Abraham Lincoln and the Civil War*. New York: Dutton Children's Books, 1997.

Weinberg, Larry, and Tom LaPadula. *The Story of Abraham Lincoln: President for the People*. Milwaukee: Gareth Stevens Pub., 1997.

Yancey, Diane. *Leaders of the North and South*. San Diego: Lucent Books, 2000.

Look for more Signature Lives
books about this era:

Jefferson Davis: *President of the Confederate States of America*

Frederick Douglass: *Slave, Writer, Abolitionist*

William Lloyd Garrison: *Abolitionist and Journalist*

Ulysses S. Grant: *Union General and U.S. President*

Thomas "Stonewall" Jackson: *Confederate General*

Robert E. Lee: *Confederate Commander*

Harriet Beecher Stowe: *Author and Advocate*

Elizabeth Van Lew: *Civil War Spy*

ON THE WEB

For more information on *Abraham Lincoln*, use FactHound to track down Web sites related to this book.

1. Go to *www.facthound.com*
2. Type in a search word related to this book or this book ID: 0756509866
3. Click on the *Fetch It* button.

FactHound will find the best Web sites for you.

HISTORIC SITES

The Abraham Lincoln Presidential Library and Museum
112 N. Sixth St.
Springfield, IL 62701
217/558-8882
To learn more about Abraham Lincoln and the era in which he lived

Lincoln Memorial
900 Ohio Drive S.W.
Washington, DC 20024
202/426-6841
To visit the memorial dedicated to the president who saved the Union

abolitionists
people who worked to get rid of slavery

accomplices
partners in doing something that is wrong

assassin
a person who murders someone well known or important, such as a president

bunting
loosely woven fabric used for decorations and flags

conspirators
people who make an agreement in secret to do something illegal

indentured servant
a person who must work for someone for a certain amount of time in return for payment of travel and living costs

inferior
of lesser importance or value

legacy
something left behind for others after a person dies

legislature
the part of government that makes or changes laws

militia
military force, often made up of local volunteers

premonition
a feeling that something is going to happen, usually bad

rebellion
an armed uprising against the government

repeal
to do away with something officially, such as a law

resuscitate
to bring back from a near-death condition

siege
the surrounding of a city or place to cut off supplies

tuberculosis
a serious bacterial disease that affects the lungs

typhoid
a serious disease carried by lice that causes a high fever, confusion, and a dark red rash

Chapter 1

Page 10, line 8: "The Emancipation Proclamation." *U.S. National Archives and Records Administration.* http://www.archives.gov/exhibit_hall/featured_documents/emancipation_proclamation/

Page 13, line 16: Russell Freedman. *Lincoln: A Photobiography.* New York: Clarion Books, 1987, p. 91.

Chapter 2

Page 25, line 20: David Herbert Donald. *Lincoln.* New York: Simon & Schuster, 1995, p. 27.

Page 26, line 24: Ibid., p. 28.

Page 27, line 19: Ibid., p. 29.

Chapter 3

Page 33, line 26: Ibid., p. 44.

Page 34, line 15: Ibid., p. 47.

Chapter 4

Page 39, line 8: Ibid., p. 58.

Page 42, line 1: Ruth Painter Randall. *I Mary: A Biography of the Girl Who Married Abraham Lincoln.* Boston: Little, Brown & Company, 1959, p. 47.

Page 43, line 20: Ibid., p. 60.

Chapter 5

Page 52, line 1: Abraham Lincoln, Paul M. Angle, and Earl Schenck Miers. *The Living Lincoln: The Man, His Mind, His Times, and the War He Fought, Reconstructed from His Own Writings.* New York: Barnes & Noble Books, 1992, p. 161.

Page 54, line 1: Ibid., p. 212.

Page 57, line 24: *I Mary: A Biography of the Girl Who Married Abraham Lincoln*, p. 136.

Chapter 6

Page 61, line 18: David Herbert Donald. *Lincoln at Home: Two Glimpses of Abraham Lincoln's Family Life.* New York: Simon & Schuster, 1999, p. 36.

Page 63, line 16: Ibid., p. 31.

Page 67, line 8: Ibid., p. 43.

Chapter 7

Page 70, sidebar: "A Nation Divided: The U.S. Civil War 1861-1865." *The History Place.* http://www.historyplace.com/civilwar/

Page 71, line 2: *Lincoln: A Photobiography*, p. 79.

Page 74, line 10: *The Living Lincoln: The Man, His Mind, His Times, and the War He Fought, Reconstructed from His Own Writings*, p. 567-568.

Page 75, line 1: Ibid., p. 591.

Page 76, line 5: Ibid.

Page 79, line 1: Ibid., p. 646.

Page 79, line 17: *Lincoln*, p. 15.

Chapter 8

Page 88, line 5: Ibid., p. 599.

Chapter 9

Page 95, line 19: *Lincoln: A Photobiography*, p. 5.

Donald, David Herbert. *Lincoln*. New York, Simon & Schuster, 1995.

Donald, David Herbert. *Lincoln at Home: Two Glimpses of Abraham Lincoln's Family Life*. New York: Simon & Schuster, 1999.

Freedman, Russell. Lincoln: *A Photobiography*. New York: Clarion Books, 1987.

Library of Congress

Lincoln, Abraham, Paul M. Angle, and Earl Schenck Miers. *The Living Lincoln: The Man, His Mind, His Times, and the War He Fought, Reconstructed from His Own Writings*. New York: Barnes & Noble Books, 1992.

National Archives and Records Administration

Randall, Ruth Painter. *I Mary: A Biography of the Girl Who Married Abraham Lincoln*. Boston: Little, Brown & Company, 1959.

The White House Web site. http://www.whitehouse.gov

13th Amendment, 72

abolitionist movement, 11, 69, 95
American Indians. *See* Native
     Americans.
Appomattox Court House, Virginia, 78,
     82
Atlanta, Georgia, 77
Atzerodt, George, 91

Bates, Edward, 71
Battle of Antietam, 70, 72
Battle of Gettysburg, 72, 74, 76
Battle of Mobile Bay, 77
Bell, John, 56
Berry, William, 34
"blab school," 19
Black Hawk (Sauk chief), 32
Black Hawk War, 32, 33
Boone, Daniel, 15, 16
Booth, John Wilkes, 82–84, 86, 89–90
Boy Scouts, 16
Breckinridge, John, 56
Burnside, Ambrose E., 70

civil rights movement, 94
Civil War, 9, 60, 65, 67, 69–70,
     72–74, 76–77, 82, 88–89
Confederate States of America, 60,
     69, 72
Constitution of the United States, 72
Constitutional Union party, 56

Davis, Jefferson, 60, 70
Decatur, Illinois, 32
Declaration of Independence, 13, 52,
     54
Democratic Party, 55–56
Douglas, Stephen, 37, 41, 43, 50, 53,
     54, 55
Douglass, Frederick, 95
Dred Scott case, 12

Edwards, Elizabeth, 41

electoral college, 57
Elizabethtown, Kentucky, 16, 17, 26
Emancipation Proclamation, 9, 10,
     13, 71, 72
Everett, Edward, 74
Executive Mansion. *See* White House.

Farragut, David, 77
First Battle of Bull Run, 69–70
Ford's Theatre, 82, 84, 85–86
Fort Sumter, 65
Founding Fathers, 12
Fox Indians, 32
Francis, Simeon, 43
Franklin, Benjamin, 27

Gentry, Allen, 30, 31
Gentry, James, 30
Gettysburg, Pennsylvania, 72
Globe Tavern, 45
Grant, Ulysses S., 73–74, 76, 78
Grigsby, Aaron, 26

"Hail to the Chief" (song), 85
Hanks, Dennis (cousin), 22
Hardin County, Kentucky, 16
Harris, Clara, 85
Herold, David, 91
Hodgenville, Kentucky, 16, 17

"I Have a Dream" speech (Martin
     Luther King Jr.), 94
Illinois, 10, 11, 32, 33-34, 39-40, 47,
     57, 89
indentured servants, 12
Indiana, 19–20, 22, 31

Johnson, Andrew, 84
Johnston, Elizabeth, 26
Johnston, John, 26
Johnston, Matilda, 26
Johnston, Sarah Bush (stepmother),
     25–27

Kansas-Nebraska Act, 50
Kentucky, 15, 16, 17, 26
King, Martin Luther, Jr., 94
Knob Creek farm, 18

Lee, Robert E., 70, 72, 78
Lincoln, Abraham
  animals and, 21, 23
  antislavery speeches by, 51–52, 54
  assassination attempts on, 67, 82, 86
  as assistant surveyor, 35–36, 37
  at Berry-Lincoln general store, 34, 47
  birth of, 18
  campaign for Illinois state legislature,
    33, 34, 37
  campaign for presidency, 55, 56–57
  campaign for U.S. Senate, 53–55
  childhood of, 18–19, 20–21,
    22–23, 25
  death of, 88
  education of, 19, 26–27, 35–36, 37,
    71
  Emancipation Proclamation and,
    9, 10, 13, 71, 72
  as farmhand, 29, 34
  flatboat trips to New Orleans, 30–31,
    32–33
  at Ford's Theatre, 85–86
  Gettysburg address, 74–76
  health of, 43, 65, 86–87
  humor of, 67, 79
  in Illinois militia, 33–34
  in Illinois state legislature, 37
  as lawyer, 37, 40, 47, 49
  letters to, 62–63, 81
  marriage of, 45
  at Offutt general store, 33
  physical description of, 29
  as postmaster, 34–35, 37
  premonitions of, 84
  as president, 9, 13, 59, 60–63, 65–67,
    69, 70–71, 72, 74–76, 77, 79, 81,
    83, 95
  Reconstruction and, 74, 79

slavery and, 12, 50–52, 56, 59
  as storyteller, 31–32
  in U.S. House of Representatives, 10,
    47
Lincoln, Abraham (grandfather), 15
Lincoln, Edward Baker "Eddie" (son),
    47, 65
Lincoln, Josiah (uncle), 15–16
Lincoln, Mary Todd (wife), 40–45,
    46–47, 61, 63, 65, 67, 81, 82, 84,
    85, 86, 87, 88, 89
Lincoln Memorial, 93–94
Lincoln, Mordecai (uncle), 15–16
Lincoln, Nancy Hanks (mother), 16–17,
    23, 24–25
Lincoln, Robert Todd (son), 45, 46, 87
Lincoln, Sarah (sister), 17, 25, 26
Lincoln, Thomas (brother), 18
Lincoln, Thomas (father), 16,
    18, 19–20, 21, 25–26, 29, 30
Lincoln, Thomas "Tad" (son), 47,
    63–64, 87
Lincoln, William Wallace "Willie"
    (son), 47, 63–65, 89
Lincoln-Douglas debates, 54–55
Little Pigeon Creek, Indiana, 20

Macon County, Illinois, 32
Maine, 50
McClellan, George, 77
Meade, George G., 70, 72
Mill Creek farm, 16
Missouri, 50
Missouri Compromise, 50, 51, 53

National Intelligencer newspaper, 79
Native Americans, 32
Nebraska, 50
New Orleans, Louisiana, 30–31
New Salem, Illinois, 33, 47
Nolin Creek farm, 17–18

Oak Ridge Cemetery, 89
Offutt, Denton, 33

Our American Cousin (play), 84

Powell, Lewis, 91

Rathbone, Henry, 85
Reconstruction, 74, 79
Republican Party, 12, 55
reservations, 32
Richmond, Virginia, 60
Rutledge, Ann, 39

Sangamon River, 32
Sauk Indians, 32
Savannah, Georgia, 77
Scott, Dred, 12
secession, 12, 59–60
settlers, 19, 32
Seward, William, 84, 85
Sherman, William T., 77
slavery, 10–11, 13, 19, 30–31, 49–50,
    50–53, 72, 82

Sparrow, Elizabeth (aunt), 22, 24
Sparrow, Thomas (uncle), 22, 24
Speed, Joshua, 40
Springfield, Illinois, 39–40, 57, 89
Stanton, Edwin M., 90
Stephens, Alexander, 60
Stuart, John, 40, 43
Surratt, Mary, 91

Todd, Robert (father-in-law), 45–46

U.S. House of Representatives, 47
U.S. Senate, 53–54, 55

Vandalia, Illinois, 40
Vicksburg, Mississippi, 74

War Department, 66–67
Washington, George, 27
White House, 61, 63, 78–79
white snakeroot plant, 23–24

Brenda Haugen started in the newspaper business and had a career as an award-winning journalist before finding her niche as an author. Since then, she has written and edited many books, most of them for children. A graduate of the University of North Dakota in Grand Forks, Brenda lives in North Dakota with her family.

Image Credits

U.S. Senate Collection/*First Reading of the Emancipation Proclamation of President Lincoln* by Francis Bicknell Carpenter, cover (top), 4–5, 11, 101 (top left); U.S. Senate Collection/*Abraham Lincoln* by Freeman Thorpe, cover (bottom), 2; Stock Montage/Getty Images, 8, 51; Library of Congress, 14, 18, 33, 56, 58, 64, 68, 71, 88, 94, 97 (top right), 98 (bottom right), 99 (bottom), 100 (top middle and bottom), 101 (bottom); North Wind Picture Archives, 17, 21, 27, 53, 96 (top); Courtesy of Picture History, 22, 41, 42; The Granger Collection, New York, 23, 31, 46, 77, 78, 85, 97 (top left); MPI/Getty Images, 28, 60, 100 (top right); James P. Rowan, 35; Abraham Lincoln Collectibles/Robert E. Church, Collection, 36; Bettmann/Corbis, 38, 44, 55, 66, 87, 98 (top), 100 (top left), 101 (top right); The Corcoran Gallery of Art/Corbis, 48, 99 (top); Corbis, 62, 90; Library of Congress/Getty Images, 75; Mary Evans Picture Library, 80; Alexander Gardner/George Eastman House/Getty Images, 83; Photodisc, 92, 96 (bottom); Evans/Three Lions/Getty Images, 97 (bottom); Texas State Library & Archives Commission, 98 (bottom left).